WE ARE ALL DIFFERENT!

That's wonderful! Some differences are easy to see. For example; different hair colour, eye colour, height and skin colour.

Other differences can't be seen.
For example; our thoughts,
feelings,
a headache, or our special skills!

MY AWESOME AUTISM

Nikki Saunders

A LWAYS

U NIQUE

T ALENTED

I NTELLIGENT

S UPER

M AGNIFICENT

Autism is a beautiful and unique gift to you, and everyone around you.

Our brains all work differently. Look at the picture! Some people see a rabbit first, some people may see a duck! What can you see?

The brain interprets how we feel.
(It gets a signal to help us understand
a situation) For example; I don't like
bright lights or very noisy places,
so my senses tell my brain and
then I start to feel my emotions.

have strong senses!
These can be smells, taste, good and bad
energies, or how our clothing feels,
soft or itchy etc.)

The special way a brain with autism work means you may be EXCEPTIONALLY skilled at something! We are all different and have different talents!

YOU ARE AMAZING!

You're amazing like me!

We all have strengths and weaknesses.

There are things that an autistic person can do, that other people find tricky. Equally other people can do things that I find tricky. That's okay.

My mummy is good at baking cakes but isn't very good at drawing!

My little brother is good at running, but isn't good at waiting for me, yet.

I can talk a lot, but some of my friends cannot. I am using sign language, to say thank you to my friend Sally, for the yummy ice cream!

Sometimes I might copy a phrase from a film or a game to explain what I need. For example "abort mission" is from my favourite computer game.

Sometimes I like to play with friends, and other times, I like to play alone and line up my toys. This is my calm place.

I do not like it when my plans or routines change.
I like to know what I am doing next.
Some children may like photos to help them.

GETTING UP

EATING BREAKFAST

Parents, family and teachers are able to support or help me learn about autism. Others can learn about it too.
As time goes on I may ask more questions.

We can all have difficulties amongst friends and talking to each other. When I get stuck or confused, I can ask my mum or a teacher to help me.

When someone asks me "what is autism?",
I just say "you can go the library and read a book about
it if you like."

YOU ARE SO LOVED

We all have different hobbies and interests. Isn't that great!
You are kind, loving and so loved by your family and friends too.

Remember, be super proud of you and celebrate how wonderful you are! Your friends and family love and care about you so much! They are SO proud of you! Stay awesome! Love Eddie.

Printed in Great Britain
by Amazon